The Old and New
World Order

Jagdish Krishanlal Arora

THE OLD AND NEW WORLD ORDER

BY

JAGDISH KRISHANLAL ARORA

This is a work of fiction. Similarities to real people, places, or events are entirely coincidental.

THE OLD AND NEW WORLD ORDER

First edition. September 26, 2023.

Copyright © 2023 Jagdish Krishanlal Arora.

Written by Jagdish Krishanlal Arora.

Table of Contents

CHAPTER ONE
The Old-World Order and its Decline

The Old-World order, particularly during the 20th century, was largely dominated by Western powers, with the United States at the forefront. This period was characterized by several key characteristics and power structures:

Superpower Dominance: The United States and the Soviet Union emerged as superpowers after World War II, with the U.S. representing the Western bloc and the Soviet Union representing the Eastern bloc. This bipolar power structure defined much of the global dynamics during the Cold War era. The United States, in particular, was the undisputed leader of the Western world.

Economic Hegemony: Western powers, led by the United States, held significant economic dominance. The Bretton Woods institutions, such as the International Monetary Fund (IMF) and the World Bank, were established under Western leadership to shape the global financial system. The U.S. dollar became the world's primary reserve currency, solidifying American economic influence.

Military Alliances: Western powers, particularly the United States, formed strong military alliances like NATO (North Atlantic Treaty Organization) to counter the perceived threat from the Eastern bloc. These alliances solidified Western military dominance and allowed for collective security.

Cultural Influence: Western culture, including music, film, fashion, and consumer products, permeated the globe. Hollywood, in particular, played a significant role in shaping global entertainment and culture. English became the de facto international language.

Colonial Legacy: Many Western powers had previously established colonial empires across Asia, Africa, and the Middle East. The legacy of colonialism, including borders drawn arbitrarily and enduring political instability in post-colonial nations, continued to shape global geopolitics.

Global Governance: International institutions like the United Nations (UN) were created with significant Western influence. The United States, as a permanent member of the UN Security Council, held considerable veto power.

Nuclear Deterrence: The development of nuclear weapons by Western powers, most notably the United States, contributed to the strategy of mutually assured destruction (MAD). This created a tense global balance of power during the Cold War, preventing major conflicts between superpowers.

Market Capitalism: Western powers championed market capitalism and the free-market economic system. The Washington Consensus, which advocated for free-market policies and economic liberalization, influenced economic policies around the world.

Interventionism: Western powers, particularly the United States, engaged in military interventions and covert operations in various parts of the world to protect perceived interests, often under the banner of containing communism during the Cold War.

The power structures of the old world order were characterized by Western dominance, with the United States serving as the primary driver of this order. However, it's essential to acknowledge that this dominance also led to criticisms and challenges. Critics argued that Western powers often pursued their interests at the expense of sovereignty and self-determination in other nations, contributing to geopolitical tensions and conflicts. The old-world order eventually underwent significant changes, including the dissolution of the Soviet Union, the rise of new global powers like China, and shifts in economic and political influence. These changes have continued to reshape the global power landscape in the 21st century.

The old-world order, dominated by Western powers, particularly the United States, had a profound impact on international relations, global governance, and economic systems throughout much of the 20th century. Here's how it shaped these aspects:

1. International Relations:

Bipolar Dynamics: The Cold War rivalry between the United States and the Soviet Union defined international relations during this era. The bipolar power structure influenced the behaviour of nations as they aligned themselves with one of the superpowers, leading to regional conflicts and proxy wars.

Military Alliances: The formation of military alliances like NATO and the Warsaw Pact solidified the power blocs led by Western and Eastern superpowers. These alliances served as instruments of deterrence and collective defence, shaping global security dynamics.

Nuclear Deterrence: The development of nuclear weapons by Western powers, especially the United States, led to a precarious balance of power. The fear of mutually assured destruction (MAD) discouraged direct military confrontation between superpowers.

Interventionism: Western powers, particularly the United States, engaged in interventions and covert operations to protect their interests and contain the spread of communism. This interventionist approach influenced foreign policy decisions worldwide.

Decolonization: The old-world order oversaw the decolonization of many African and Asian nations. Western powers, while granting independence to former colonies, often left behind political, economic, and social legacies that shaped post-colonial dynamics.

2. Global Governance:

Founding of International Institutions: The United States played a pivotal role in establishing international organizations like the United Nations (UN), the International Monetary Fund (IMF), and the World Bank. These institutions aimed to foster cooperation, maintain peace, and provide economic stability.

Security Council Dominance: The UN Security Council, with its five permanent members, including the United States, held significant power in global governance. This structure allowed Western powers to influence and, at times, veto key decisions.

Economic Hegemony: Western powers dominated the global financial system. The U.S. dollar became the world's primary reserve currency, and the Bretton Woods institutions promoted Western economic interests and values.

Cultural Influence: Western culture, driven by the United States, had a substantial impact on global culture, from music and movies to fashion and consumer trends. English became the lingua franca of international diplomacy.

3. Economic Systems:

Market Capitalism: Western powers championed market capitalism and free-market economic systems. This ideology influenced economic policies around the world, promoting privatization, deregulation, and trade liberalization.

Bretton Woods Institutions: The IMF and the World Bank, established by Western powers, played central roles in stabilizing the global economy and providing financial assistance to nations in need. However, they were also criticized for imposing Western economic policies on recipient countries.

Global Trade: The old world order facilitated a surge in global trade, led by Western powers. The General Agreement on Tariffs and Trade (GATT) and later the World Trade Organization (WTO) promoted free trade and economic integration.

While the old-world order brought relative stability and economic growth to many Western nations, it also faced criticism for perpetuating inequality, neocolonialism, and interventionism in other regions. This order began to evolve with the dissolution of the Soviet Union, the emergence of new global players like China, and shifting economic and political dynamics in the late 20th century. These changes have continued to reshape international relations, global governance, and economic systems in the 21st century.

The old -world order began to decline significantly in the late 20th century, marked by several key events and conflicts. One of the most significant turning points was the end of the Cold War, but other events also contributed to the erosion of the old order. Here are some key events:

End of the Cold War (1989-1991): The Cold War, characterized by the rivalry between the United States and the Soviet Union, came to an end in 1989-1991. The collapse of the Berlin Wall in 1989 symbolized the reunification of East and West Germany and the beginning of the end of the division of Europe. In 1991, the Soviet Union itself dissolved, leading to the emergence of newly independent states in Eastern Europe and Central Asia. The end of the Cold War marked a significant shift in global power dynamics, as the bipolar world order gave way to a unipolar system with the United States as the sole superpower.

Gulf War (1990-1991): The Gulf War, triggered by Iraq's invasion of Kuwait in 1990, highlighted the limitations of the old world order in addressing new conflicts. A U.S.-led coalition intervened to liberate Kuwait, demonstrating the United States' military dominance. This conflict also exposed fractures within the UN Security Council, as not all permanent members supported the intervention.

Rise of China: China's economic and geopolitical rise, particularly in the late 20th and early 21st centuries, challenged the Western-dominated old order. China's economic reforms, rapid growth, and expanding global influence signalled the emergence of a new power centre. Its entry into the World Trade Organization in 2001 further solidified its position in the global economic system.

Post-Cold War Conflicts: The post-Cold War era witnessed a series of conflicts and crises, including the breakup of Yugoslavia and the Balkan Wars, the Rwandan Genocide, and the humanitarian intervention in Kosovo. These events tested the international community's ability to respond effectively to crises without the Cold War's clear power structures.

Globalization: Advances in technology and communication led to increased globalization, with the flow of information, capital, and people across borders. This trend challenged traditional notions of sovereignty and economic control, making it harder for Western powers to maintain dominance.

9/11 and the War on Terror: The September 11, 2001 terrorist attacks in the United States ushered in a new era of international relations. The U.S.-led War on Terror, including the wars in Afghanistan and Iraq, marked a significant shift in global power dynamics and strained alliances. These conflicts revealed the limits of military intervention and raised questions about the legitimacy of unilateral actions.

Financial Crisis (2008): The global financial crisis of 2008 exposed vulnerabilities in the Western-dominated economic system. It led to increased scrutiny of Western financial institutions and raised questions about the stability of the global economic order.

These events, among others, signalled the decline of the old-world order characterized by Western dominance, the end of the Cold War, and the emergence of new global dynamics. The 21st century has seen the continued evolution of international relations, global governance, and economic systems as new powers have risen and traditional structures have adapted to a changing world.

CHAPTER TWO
New World Order

The New World Order is an imaginary concept. I had read about it many years back don't exactly remember when. This world order many think is pre-planned and run by secret cults who control the world directly and indirectly. Many a times I thought this should be hidden but with several restrictions in many different countries for travel and access to authentic information I have though to explain everything about this New World Order. The New World Order is also a result of China, Russia and India becoming more powerful economically and in global trade resulting in addition of more powers to the already crowded market of rich countries. Therefore, with new found money, these countries also want a slice in the control of the people of Earth using their huge money reserves earned through global trade.

Whenever Kings in olden times became rich through taxes, they invaded other countries, stole and looted property of the people of those countries and expanded their kingdoms. The entire landscape of occupied countries changed. Today it is not easy to invade and occupy countries, but still some countries try to do so, with heavy losses in the end. But the quest continues and most of it is dared by Dictators who want to retain false older glory, but they forget the old grand nations were also a result of invading and occupying other countries forcefully and those countries were never a part of Russia, Afghanistan, Britian, Greece, Persia or any other country. Tomorrow when populations increase, we may even switch over to having lot of smaller countries as before, where countries like India were 565 small and big kingdoms each with its own language and kings.

The shift from the old-world order to the new world order is characterized by several factors that have reshaped the global geopolitical landscape. Key contributors to this shift include the rise of China, the resurgence of Russia, and the changing role of the United States:

Rise of China

Economic Ascendancy: China's economic transformation over the past few decades has been nothing short of remarkable. Its rapid industrialization, export-led growth, and massive population have made it the world's second-largest economy. China's integration into the global supply chain has disrupted traditional economic power structures.

Global Trade and Investment: China's Belt and Road Initiative (BRI), a massive infrastructure and trade network, has expanded its influence across Asia, Europe, Africa, and beyond. It has allowed China to extend its economic reach and establish closer ties with numerous nations.

Diplomatic Influence: China's diplomatic efforts have expanded its influence in international organizations. It has become a major player in forums like the United Nations and has been active in shaping global governance on issues such as climate change and sustainable development.

Military Modernization: China's military modernization, particularly its naval capabilities, has raised concerns among neighbouring nations and global powers. It has sought to assert its territorial claims in the South China Sea, leading to regional tensions.

Resurgence of Russia

Reassertion of Influence: Russia, under the leadership of Vladimir Putin, has pursued a more assertive foreign policy. It has sought to regain influence in former Soviet states and neighbouring regions, notably in Ukraine and Georgia.

Military Interventions: Russia's military interventions in Crimea, Ukraine, and Syria have challenged the post-Cold War order and raised questions about the sanctity of international borders. These actions have strained relations with Western powers.

Energy Dominance: Russia's vast energy resources, particularly its natural gas exports to Europe, have given it significant economic leverage and political influence in the region. This energy dominance has allowed it to maintain a strong position in global affairs.

Changing Role of the United States:

Relative Decline: While the United States remains a global superpower, its relative economic and geopolitical influence has declined compared to the post-World War II era. The rise of other powers, particularly China, has shifted the global balance of power.

Evolving Foreign Policy: U.S. foreign policy priorities have evolved, with a greater emphasis on domestic issues, counterterrorism, and competition with peer competitors like China. The U.S. has also experienced shifts in its international alliances and commitments.

Multilateralism and Alliances: The United States has sought to rebuild and strengthen alliances, particularly in response to rising powers and global challenges like climate change and cybersecurity. It has reengaged with international organizations and agreements.

Challenges to Global Leadership: The perception of U.S. leadership has faced challenges, both internally and externally. Issues such as political polarization, economic inequality, and the handling of international crises have led to questions about the effectiveness of U.S. leadership.

These factors, among others, have contributed to the shift from the old world order to the new world order. This evolving global landscape is characterized by a multipolar distribution of power, where multiple actors, including rising powers, have greater influence in shaping international relations, global governance, and economic systems. The dynamics of this new world order continue to evolve and will shape global affairs in the 21st century.

Globalization, technology, and climate change are three interconnected forces that play a significant role in shaping the new world order. Each presents both challenges and opportunities that have far-reaching implications for international relations, governance, and the global economy:

1. Globalization

Challenges:

Economic Inequality: Globalization has contributed to economic growth but has also exacerbated income inequality, both within and between countries. This disparity can lead to social and political tensions.

Job Displacement: The outsourcing of jobs to lower-wage countries and automation driven by globalization can lead to job displacement in high-wage nations, causing economic anxiety and political backlash.

Dependency and Vulnerability: Some nations have become highly dependent on global supply chains for essential goods, making them vulnerable to disruptions, such as the COVID-19 pandemic.

Opportunities:

Economic Growth: Globalization can lead to increased economic growth, trade, and investment, benefiting nations and reducing poverty when managed effectively.

Cultural Exchange: It facilitates cultural exchange and understanding among nations, fostering tolerance and diversity.

Global Problem-Solving: Globalization enables cooperation on global issues like public health, climate change, and security, as challenges often transcend national borders.

2. Technology

Challenges:

Digital Divide: Access to technology is not evenly distributed globally, creating a digital divide that exacerbates existing inequalities and limits opportunities for some populations.

Cybersecurity Threats: The proliferation of digital technology has led to increased cyber threats, including hacking, cyber espionage, and ransomware attacks, which pose security risks to nations and organizations.

Privacy Concerns: The collection and use of personal data by technology companies have raised concerns about privacy and data security.

Opportunities

Innovation: Technology drives innovation in various sectors, from healthcare to renewable energy, and can address complex global challenges.

Global Connectivity: Technology enables instant global communication and cooperation, making it easier to coordinate responses to crises and facilitate international collaboration.

Economic Growth: The technology sector itself contributes significantly to economic growth and job creation.

3. Climate Change

Challenges:

Environmental Degradation: Climate change leads to environmental degradation, affecting ecosystems, biodiversity, and the availability of natural resources.

Economic Impacts: Extreme weather events, rising sea levels, and disruptions to agriculture and supply chains can have significant economic consequences, particularly for vulnerable nations.

Migration and Conflict: Climate-induced migration and resource scarcity can lead to displacement and exacerbate conflicts over water, land, and other resources.

Opportunities

Renewable Energy Transition: The shift to renewable energy sources can reduce greenhouse gas emissions, create jobs, and stimulate green technology innovation.

International Cooperation: Climate change necessitates international cooperation, fostering diplomacy and alliances among nations to address this global challenge.

Innovation: Climate change mitigation and adaptation efforts drive technological innovation and investment in sustainable practices.

Globalization, technology, and climate change are pivotal forces that are profoundly shaping the new world order. The challenges they pose, such as economic inequality, cybersecurity threats, and environmental degradation, require careful global management. However, they also offer opportunities for economic growth, cultural exchange, innovation, and international cooperation. The ability of nations and international organizations to navigate these complexities will greatly influence the future trajectory of global governance, economic systems, and international relations.

CHAPTER THREE
Role of the United Nations, WTO, NATO and European Union in the New World Order

International institutions like the United Nations (UN), World Trade Organization (WTO), European Union and NATO have played critical roles in adapting to the evolving global landscape. Each institution has faced unique challenges and opportunities as they seek to remain relevant and effective in a changing world. Britian strongly opposes joining the European Union as it diminishes its role as a major colonial power, which it is no longer in existence as on today.

United Nations (UN):

Challenges

Security Council Reform: One of the most significant challenges for the UN has been reforming the UN Security Council to reflect contemporary power dynamics. The current structure, established after World War II, does not accurately represent the distribution of power in the 21st century.

Complex Global Conflicts: The UN has had to respond to increasingly complex and protracted conflicts, often involving non-state actors and asymmetric warfare. These conflicts pose challenges to traditional peacekeeping and conflict resolution efforts.

Resource Constraints: The UN's effectiveness has sometimes been limited by resource constraints and financial dependencies on major member states.

Adaptations

Conflict Prevention and Mediation: The UN has increasingly focused on conflict prevention and mediation efforts, recognizing the importance of addressing conflicts before they escalate into crises.

Global Goals: The adoption of the Sustainable Development Goals (SDGs) in 2015 has provided a framework for addressing global challenges, including poverty, inequality, and climate change, and aligning the UN's activities with broader international priorities.

Partnerships: The UN has formed partnerships with regional organizations and non-governmental actors to enhance its effectiveness in addressing complex global issues.

World Trade Organization (WTO)

Challenges:

Stalled Negotiations: The WTO has faced difficulties in advancing global trade negotiations, including the Doha Development Round. Deadlocks in negotiations have raised questions about its ability to adapt to changing economic dynamics.

Economic Disparities: The WTO has struggled to address economic disparities between developed and developing countries, with concerns about the impact of trade liberalization on vulnerable industries and workers.

Emerging Trade Issues: The WTO has had to address new trade challenges, such as e-commerce, digital trade, and intellectual property, which were not well-covered by existing agreements.

Adaptations

Plurilateral Agreements: The WTO has pursued plurilateral agreements, where subsets of members agree to specific trade rules. This approach allows for more flexible negotiations on certain issues.

E-commerce Negotiations: The initiation of negotiations on e-commerce and digital trade has reflected an effort to address contemporary trade challenges.

Support for Developing Nations: Efforts have been made to provide technical assistance and capacity-building to developing nations to help them engage more effectively in the global trading system.

NATO (North Atlantic Treaty Organization)

Challenges:

Changing Security Threats: NATO has had to adapt to new security challenges, including cyber threats, hybrid warfare, and regional conflicts outside the alliance's traditional area of operation.

Alliance Cohesion: Maintaining the cohesion of the alliance among diverse member states with varying strategic priorities has been a challenge, especially in the face of shifting geopolitical dynamics.

U.S. Commitment: Questions about the United States' commitment to NATO have arisen, leading to concerns about the alliance's future.

Adaptations:

Enhanced Cyber Defence: NATO has recognized the importance of cybersecurity and has established cyber defence as a core mission.

Partnerships: NATO has expanded partnerships with non-member states and organizations to address shared security challenges.

Increased Focus on Collective Defence: The alliance has renewed its focus on collective defence and deterrence, with a commitment to maintaining military capabilities and readiness.

The European Union (EU) is a political and economic union of 27 European countries that are located primarily in Europe. It is one of the most significant and ambitious regional integration projects in history. Here are some key aspects of the European Union:

1. History and Origins:

The origins of the EU can be traced back to the aftermath of World War II when European leaders sought to prevent another devastating conflict on the continent.

The European Coal and Steel Community (ECSC) and the European Economic Community (EEC) were formed in the 1950s as precursors to the EU. The Treaty of Rome in 1957 established the EEC, creating a common market for goods and services among its founding members.

Over the years, the EU has expanded its membership, starting with six founding members and now comprising 27 member states after the United Kingdom's withdrawal in 2020 (commonly referred to as Brexit).

2. Institutions:

The EU has several key institutions, including the European Commission, the European Parliament, the Council of the European Union, the European Council, and the Court of Justice of the European Union. These institutions play various roles in shaping and implementing EU policies.

3. Single Market and Currency:

One of the EU's primary achievements is the establishment of a single market, which allows for the free movement of goods, services, capital, and people among member states.

The Euro (€) is the official currency of the Eurozone, which includes 19 EU member states. It has become one of the world's major reserve currencies.

4. Common Policies:

The EU has developed common policies in various areas, including agriculture, competition, trade, environment, and consumer protection. These policies are designed to harmonize regulations and create a level playing field among member states.

5. Enlargement:

The EU has expanded its membership through a series of enlargement rounds. Candidate countries must meet specific criteria, including political stability, adherence to democratic values, and the ability to adopt EU laws and regulations.

6. Foreign Policy and Diplomacy:

The EU conducts a common foreign and security policy (CFSP) to promote peace and stability in the world. It also has a High Representative for Foreign Affairs and Security Policy who represents the EU on the global stage.

7. Challenges:

The EU has faced numerous challenges, including economic crises (such as the Eurozone crisis), migration and refugee flows, and internal political divisions among member states.

Brexit, the UK's decision to leave the EU, was a significant setback for the union but also highlighted the complexities of member state relationships.

8. Future Integration:

The EU continues to discuss and debate further integration, including deeper economic and monetary union, defence cooperation, and shared decision-making in key policy areas.

9. Role on the Global Stage:

The EU is a major player in international relations, promoting multilateralism, human rights, and addressing global challenges such as climate change. It is one of the world's largest economies and trading blocs.

The European Union represents a unique experiment in regional cooperation and integration. It has contributed to decades of peace in Europe and has played a significant role in shaping the political, economic, and social landscape of the continent. However, it also faces ongoing challenges as it seeks to address issues like economic disparities, populism, and the balance between national sovereignty and supranational governance.

International institutions like the UN, WTO, EU, and NATO have been proactive in adapting to the evolving global landscape. They have addressed challenges by reforming their approaches, embracing new issues, and fostering cooperation with a broader range of actors. While these institutions continue to face significant challenges, their adaptability and resilience remain vital in addressing global issues and maintaining international stability and cooperation.

Geopolitical Implications of the New World Order:

Shifts in Alliances: The evolving global landscape has led to shifts in alliances as nations seek to adapt to changing power dynamics. Traditional alliances, such as NATO, have faced challenges in maintaining cohesion, while new partnerships have emerged. For example, China's Belt and Road Initiative has created economic ties with numerous nations, influencing their geopolitical alignments.

Rise of Multipolarity: The new world order is marked by multipolarity, with multiple centers of power challenging the dominance of a single superpower. The United States, China, Russia, and the European Union are among the major poles of influence. This multipolarity can lead to both competition and cooperation among these powers.

Potential for Conflicts: The competition for resources, influence, and strategic advantages among major powers can increase the potential for conflicts. Geopolitical flashpoints, such as the South China Sea, Ukraine, and the Taiwan Strait, have the potential to escalate into conflicts with global implications.

Impact on Regions:

Middle East: The Middle East remains a volatile region where major powers, including the United States, Russia, and China, compete for influence. Conflicts in Syria, Yemen, and Libya have become proxy battlegrounds for these powers. Additionally, the region's energy resources continue to be a source of geopolitical importance.

Asia-Pacific: The Asia-Pacific region is a focal point of the new world order due to China's rise. Territorial disputes in the South China Sea have strained relations between China and its neighbours, particularly the United States. The region is characterized by a complex web of alliances and partnerships, with nations like Japan, South Korea, and India seeking to balance Chinese influence.

Europe: Europe faces challenges related to its security architecture, with NATO navigating tensions with Russia and seeking to adapt to new security threats. The European Union plays a crucial role in shaping the region's economic and political dynamics, aiming to maintain its unity and influence on the global stage.

Strategies Employed by Major Powers:

United States: The U.S. employs a strategy of renewed engagement with allies and multilateral organizations to strengthen its position in the new world order. It seeks to balance competition with China while addressing global challenges like climate change and cybersecurity.

China: China's Belt and Road Initiative is a cornerstone of its strategy to expand influence through economic means. It has also modernized its military to assert itself in territorial disputes and seeks to promote its own vision of global governance.

Russia: Russia employs a combination of military assertiveness, energy diplomacy, and political influence to assert itself on the global stage. It has formed alliances with countries like Syria and seeks to maintain its regional dominance in Eastern Europe.

European Union: The EU emphasizes diplomacy, economic integration, and a rules-based international order. It aims to be a global actor, particularly in addressing climate change, and is working to strengthen its defence capabilities.

In the new world order, major powers are employing a mix of diplomatic, economic, and military strategies to assert their influence. The complex interplay of these strategies, coupled with shifting alliances and multipolarity, creates a dynamic geopolitical landscape with both opportunities for cooperation and risks of conflicts that have global consequences. Managing these challenges will be a central task for policymakers in the 21st century.

Role of Technological Advancements:

AI (Artificial Intelligence): AI is shaping the new world order by transforming industries, economies, and military capabilities. Nations are competing to lead in AI research and development, as it offers advantages in areas like autonomous weapons, cybersecurity, healthcare, and economic productivity. The race for AI supremacy has become a geopolitical competition, with implications for alliances and global influence.

Cybersecurity: The increasing reliance on digital technology has made cybersecurity a critical issue. Nations are investing in cybersecurity measures to protect their critical infrastructure, data, and national security. Cyberattacks can have profound geopolitical consequences, as they blur the line between conventional and cyber warfare.

Biotechnology: Advances in biotechnology, including gene editing and synthetic biology, have raised ethical, security, and regulatory challenges. These technologies have applications in medicine, agriculture, and biodefense, and their development is closely monitored for potential misuse.

Global Response to Environmental Challenges:

Climate Change: Climate change is a pressing global challenge, prompting international agreements like the Paris Agreement. Nations are adopting renewable energy, emissions reduction targets, and climate adaptation measures. Climate diplomacy and cooperation have become central to international relations, with the potential to reshape global economic dynamics and alliances.

Resource Scarcity: Increasing resource scarcity, particularly in water and minerals, can lead to conflicts and geopolitical tensions. Competition for access to resources can affect global trade patterns and alliances. Sustainable resource management and cooperation are vital to addressing these challenges.

Intersection of Technology and Environmental Concerns with Geopolitical and Economic Dynamics:

Geopolitical Impact: Technology and environmental issues intersect with geopolitics in various ways. For example, disputes over access to rare earth minerals (essential for technology manufacturing) have geopolitical implications. Similarly, control over critical digital infrastructure and AI capabilities can shape global power dynamics.

Economic Dynamics: Technological advancements drive economic growth and innovation. Nations that lead in key technologies gain economic advantages. Meanwhile, addressing environmental challenges, such as transitioning to clean energy, can create new economic opportunities and reshape global trade patterns.

Conflict and Cooperation: Technology and environmental issues can both be sources of conflict and cooperation. Cybersecurity threats can strain relations between nations, while cooperation on climate change mitigation can foster diplomatic alliances. Additionally, emerging technologies like AI have the potential to revolutionize conflict and warfare.

International Governance: The intersection of technology and environmental concerns highlights the need for effective international governance. This includes agreements on data privacy, cybersecurity norms, and environmental regulations. International institutions play a crucial role in shaping rules and standards in these domains.

Technological advancements and environmental challenges are integral to shaping the new world order. They influence geopolitical competition, economic dynamics, conflict resolution, and international cooperation. Navigating these complex intersections requires careful diplomacy, innovation, and multilateral efforts to address the shared challenges of the 21st century.

The New World order is not knew it was there before several centuries before. Those world orders were in Christians, Muslims, Hindus, Greeks and several other civilizations and may continue in future centuries also. This New World Order automatically gets established after a major event in nature. Some of the examples of the New World Order occurring in the past are the Noah's Ark and the Ten Commandments of God and establishment of the Bible, coming of Jesus and the New Testament in Christianity.

In the Hindus the Ramayana and the Mahabharata it was the New World order during the fight with the demon king Ravan in Ramayan and the Kurushetra war in Mahabharata where they say millions died.

The coming and going of the Romans was also a New World Order and so was the coming of the Prophet Mohammed and establishment of Koran in Muslims. For the Chinese and others left out in this it was Buddhism and coming of the Buddha. It was there at the time of Greek civilizations and hundreds of other civilizations such as the Incas and others which will be difficult to discuss all at once.

So we will focus on the New World order at present situation and what is the planning how it should be implemented and this will be different from anything you know about the New World Order.

We will come back to the Old-World Order later in our book. This is how the New World Order is working. We have had several wars and pandemics and after each of these calamities we had a New World Order. It is a sort of an experiment which happens and sometimes you will feel we are doing it on purpose. But it is not that way. Whenever a war or a natural calamity like epidemic, earthquake, flood or famine takes place lot of animals get displaces which include humans as well as those animals in the forests. For us both are animals.

This cannot be called a New World Order as is being spread by some unintelligent human beings. As I said changing the old traditional values of family care, taking care of parents, family values and methods of worship are our Old-World Order.

Believing in God as the Supreme Being is the Old -World Order. Believing in what God has made, the plants, animals, oceans, rivers, ponds, lakes, mountains, hills, humans, birds, water kingdom, land kingdom, clouds, rain, sky, air, water, trees, underground creatures and the beautiful natural places and landscapes is Old World Order and God as the creator.

Definitely humans have advanced further making missiles, bombs, gun powder, wars, tanks, missiles, rockets, nuclear and atom bombs, armies, surveillance equipment's, spies, intelligence agencies, military planes, space rockets, satellites, space travel, laws, taxes, rules, governments, vehicles like trucks, cars, bikes, bicycles and communication equipment's like mobile phones, electricity, toll taxes using built own and operate methods, planes, digital transactions and purchasing of goods, identity cards of various kinds, restrictions on travel, restriction on freedom of speech, privacy and hundreds of such acts are the New World Order.

Old World Order is simple and easy to use and New World order means restriction on travel, going to schools and colleges, restriction of physical activities and unlimited restrictions, which mean all food and vegetables, come to your house including medicines and doctors. It will slowly also include lawyers coming to your house, court orders at house, court hearings online, house arrests may become common which means you will not physically stay in Jail but you activity to work will be restricted.

You will have to pay to go to work, come back and lockdowns will be common. Most of the above things are started to being implemented already, which actually is quite unbelievable as I though it may take some hundred years to start. The speed with which it is implemented is amazing.

The New World Order will stop worship of God. As in the past when we had to make everything afresh the same thing is happening that time Kings became Gods and now Politicians have become Gods although they have no roles to play. This is because government has become huge, their demands for expenditure have become very large forcing them to put more and more taxes on the innocent people tp pay salaries of an ever-increasing employee's base.

Every year the governments need to increase taxes and come out with new taxes and laws. To implement the laws and taxes they have to employ more and more people. The taxation and new laws are actually made for revenue generation and not for really helping the public. New roads and bridges mean toll taxes which are several times more than the actual costs of those structures and new taxes means accusing millions of people of crimes which were not a crime before by restricting movements of body parts and speech and writing.

These are mass revenue generation items which also include identity cards, first make the identity cards, then link them with bank accounts, then link them with property and use note ban to end all cash and convert the system to digital currency where you need not use cash and can also buy and spend money anywhere in the world.

God is aware of all this and much more and we are also worried about people going to the Moon and Mars and it is of concern to us. While God does not mind peaceful explorations of some parts of the Galaxy, he is very much worried about some of the explorations and most of you will wonder why he is silent on them and does not take action or is he sleeping.

Well God does sleep and it is his right to relax whoever he wants like we humans do. He has given us a lot of things and it is tiring to look after the planet when the humans have created huge problems for themselves in unlimited wants and desires and pleasures of the unknown. Things which were crimes earlier are now made legal by governments and those activities which were illegal have now become legal.

So freedom of speech, movement, air, water and desire to talk to anyone in any country was legal before but now water, air is bought, travel requires permission and talking to people of specific countries means punishment and speech is restricted.

Asking for identity, spying on people, tapping phones, stealing information of bank accounts, property information, and bribe collection was illegal but now it is legal and involves participation of several parties who represent the legal system. These activities existed in the past also but now have acquired demonic proportions. Toll taxes are also bribes and heavy taxes on fuels are bribes as well as unreasonable taxes are also bribing as to avoid these heavy taxes one has to pay under the nose. Penalty notices hardly lead to revenue collections and only the officer sending the penalty notice gets money and it does not transfer to the government and to recover the bribes paid to officer, the person has to multiply the crimes resulting in more wrong after passing those laws.

The person who goes to Jail become unafraid and comes back by fighting elections and becoming a lawmaker himself and amassing huge money in the process. There is an endless New World Order which will be almost impossible for me to explain and too difficult for you to read also. So, I will focus on only the important points.

The politicians who claim to resist the New World Order become slaves of it when they come to power as they find changing the system is not easy. The one who can change the system and get rid of the New World Order is put in Jail and false charges are put against him or he is put in a honey trap where some women accuses him of sexual assault or rape or he is accused of treason against his country.

Not only this the New World Order exists as a secret society with Drugs, night parties, celebrities, big politicians, rich people, famous people being part of this. Even after the New World Order these secret societies are still illegal as before as they are part of New World Order and are run by paying bribes to the Law and those from the Law are also part of those secret societies. These also include earlier Kings, Queens, Princes, Princesses and Dictators families and the rich and the wealthy businessmen and rich people who have so much money they do not need not do anything except enjoy the luxuries of life.

Definitely, the purpose of God is not to destroy the existing system in anyway but over a period of time the taxes, pollution, unlimited infrastructure, depletion of the Ozone layer, military built up, biological and nuclear weapons, restrictions on movement and freedom of speech and unlimited destruction of nature is a cause of concern and no one will listen.

So, what is the problem is no one wants to listen to God. We will not stop pollution, we will make unlimited vehicles, use maximum fuel, put unlimited taxes, ask for hundreds of identities for a single person, ask him to show all his bank accounts, cash, transactions, where he travels in his entire life, with whom he came in contact, what he has spoken with other person even if those activities are non-criminal. This is what I mean by legal activities becoming illegal.

All illegal activities like charging for travelling from one place to another like toll taxes, unwanted taxes, bribes, taxes on food, tax on writing, speaking, tax on all services, vegetables, grains, tax on moving arms and legs, selling water and air now becoming illegal are only some of those. So after paying a tax those activities become legal as long as there is a tax on them. It should be self-explanatory as explaining it in layman's term is difficult.

New World order collects taxes to finance military expansion, finance space missions, military technology, pay for an increasing workforce, building and stocking weapons of mass destruction which will only be useful to destroy the planet and everything built by God to achieve supremacy of one country over the other and increase surveillance of human beings in the name of security and hindering privacy in the process.

The question now arises is that which World Order the people want and what is good for them. Naturally, the new generation wants a fast life, life full of parties, intermingling in various forms for pleasure, new gadgets like computers, tablets, high end vehicles, digital communication, all family communications without physical meeting, no playgrounds only watch sports online no physical attendance in stadiums, online casinos, gambling, online chatting and dating and someday they may not even marry but have several friends and girlfriends online.

Ordering food online is good; no cooking in the house, eating readymade meals is also good. Converting to green like using electric cars and electric vehicles, ordering medicines online, online doctors, online schools and colleges is also good. Paying unlimited types of taxes for paying for government employees, security, militaries, military weapons, roads, bridges, railways, huge government building is also good. All this and, much more is the New World Order and we don't accept it in our Old World Order run by God.

But there is a limit to paying taxes and in the New World Order the question comes of survival of the fittest, which means only those will survive to enjoy all the New World order who can pay all the taxes, can make all the multiple identities, can keep and show all their bank accounts and transaction, show all their social media activities, show all their movements throughout their entire lives in digital form, show proofs of income or business, restrict their movements and also restrict freedom of speech. These are only some of the requirements of the New World Order.

So, you think you can do all of this, well the answer is Yes and No. All of this had existed before and God was displeased with it. The New World Order says that most of the Old-World Order System has been destroyed and is non-existent.

But even after the Old-World Order being dead, still children will be born the same old way, humans will still have eyes, ears, bones, stomach although they did try to make babies in laboratories. Had the scientist succeeded in making clones, then marriage will not be necessary, people would not want to go through the birth process and they will simply hand over the genes to the labs and produce babies and pay for it. The scientists are already trying to bring alive the dinosaurs through these means.

We eliminated dinosaurs' as they were quite big and powerful enough to kill all other forms of life including plants, animals, humans and everything on Earth. Now the humans want them back for wonder as something unique and rare.

Scientists are trying hard to master cloning and some countries did act on it and made it illegal to research, but some illegal research still goes on and now like I said people have started to find out legal methods of making illegal things legal. Now, cloning is become legal where we store the gene sequencing of humans, the gene sequencing is also a hidden form of cloning, and will acquire the same results as cloning of life forms be it humans, animals, plants, water and air animals such as fishes and birds.

Now no law against cloning works as gene sequencing and research is now illegal and considered essential. This will also become another form of business to trace people and trace their identities by making identity cards using gene information. Then comes tracing ancestry, identity theft, storing database of all genes of all humans, exchanging the information for money, cloning at some future dates and endless other possibilities.

All this may seem good at first, but wait till you hear what happens next. As things become more and more complex with gene sequencing, taxation, identity requirements, speech and travel restrictions, confinement to home, people actually find it a necessary requirement.

Someday we may even have helicopters delivering food, money, paper, goods, flying cars, government and private company employees travelling to work by helicopters and almost empty work offices.

Almost every country will have huge multistorey buildings which will be interconnected by cars travelling on rails and some countries have even implemented them.

CHAPTER FOUR
Global Challenges to the New World Order

Global Challenges Transcending Traditional Borders:

Pandemics: Infectious diseases like COVID-19 can spread rapidly across borders, posing global health threats. Pandemics not only endanger lives but also disrupt economies and strain healthcare systems.

Terrorism: Terrorism knows no boundaries and can occur in any part of the world. Terrorist groups often operate across borders, making international cooperation crucial for counterterrorism efforts.

Cyber Threats: Cyberattacks, including hacking, data breaches, and cyber espionage, can target organizations, governments, and critical infrastructure worldwide. These threats exploit the interconnected nature of the internet.

Climate Change: Climate change is a global challenge with far-reaching consequences, including rising sea levels, extreme weather events, and food and water insecurity. It transcends borders, affecting nations irrespective of their contributions to greenhouse gas emissions.

Migration: Forced displacement, driven by conflict, persecution, and environmental factors, leads to large-scale migration across borders, straining resources and infrastructure in host countries.

Need for International Cooperation:

Pandemics: Effective pandemic response requires international collaboration to share data, resources, and vaccines. Organizations like the World Health Organization (WHO) play a vital role in coordinating global responses.

Terrorism: International cooperation is essential to track and disrupt terrorist networks, share intelligence, and implement measures to prevent terrorist financing and recruitment.

Cyber Threats: Cybersecurity requires cooperation to establish norms, share threat intelligence, and coordinate responses to cyberattacks. International agreements like the Budapest Convention aim to address cybercrime.

Climate Change: Mitigating climate change demands global cooperation to reduce emissions, adapt to its impacts, and support vulnerable nations. The Paris Agreement represents a significant international effort to address this challenge.

Migration: Managing migration effectively requires cooperation to address root causes, improve border security, and ensure humanitarian treatment of migrants. International organizations like the United Nations High Commissioner for Refugees (UNHCR) work on these issues.

Effectiveness of Existing Mechanisms

Pandemics: The COVID-19 pandemic revealed both the importance of international cooperation and the limitations of existing mechanisms. Vaccine distribution and equitable access remain challenges.

Terrorism: While international cooperation has resulted in some successes, terrorism persists in various forms. Challenges include differing national interests and a lack of a unified approach.

Cyber Threats: International efforts to combat cyber threats have made progress, but challenges persist due to the lack of a binding global treaty on cybersecurity and differences in national cybersecurity strategies.

Climate Change: The Paris Agreement is seen as a significant achievement, but some nations have not met their commitments. The challenge lies in ensuring countries adhere to their pledges and increase their ambition over time.

Migration: Migration remains a contentious issue, with varying approaches and policies among nations. The effectiveness of international cooperation efforts depends on political will and shared responsibility.

Successful Collaboration and Ongoing Challenges:

Successful Collaboration: Some successes in international cooperation include the eradication of diseases like smallpox, joint counterterrorism efforts, and global agreements on environmental protection.

Ongoing Challenges: Persistent challenges include geopolitical tensions, sovereignty concerns, and a lack of enforcement mechanisms for international agreements. Achieving consensus among diverse nations can be challenging.

Global challenges that transcend traditional borders require international cooperation to address effectively. While significant progress has been made in various areas, challenges persist, and the effectiveness of cooperation mechanisms depends on the willingness of nations to work together, uphold commitments, and adapt to evolving threats. Efforts to strengthen international cooperation and address global challenges will continue to be a central aspect of the evolving new world order.

Some people consider World War I and World War II as a New World Order which took place during the pandemic of the 1920s. This is not true as the World wars were results of several other factors and some Dictators trying to gain supremacy and become sole leaders of the entire planet. A similar situation does exist today where some leaders are trying to also become leaders of other countries and even register their political parties in neighbouring countries to expand their political bases. They also invite political leaders from other countries at the time of democratic elections and then visit the other countries to make those leaders win.

This way these political leaders try to become world famous, by acting as marketing leaders for each other to make them win, outside of their own country boundaries, which is totally illegal and want entire mankind to accept them as global permanent leaders or simply as Dictators bypassing our democratic systems. They don't want to lose any elections and try to win all elections, and still show their country is democratic when in fact they have eliminated all opposition parties in their so-called democratic country. They start with becoming head of a small state within their country then become a country head, then try to become global leaders. These are extremist leaders who enjoy the support of a large section of the population like it was with Osama Bin Laden in Afghanistan and Saddam Hussein in Iraq and Hitler in Germany. Similar leaders exist in the world today, but they hide themselves behind a religious mask acting as religion friendly and also acting democratic, but their true intentions are to become Dictators like Hitler, Saddam Hussein and also powerful like Osama bin Laden having support of millions of religious extremists. The other world leaders are naturally afraid of them even after having powerful militaries. Now wars are being fought with a combination of doing business with rich western countries, earning the money from them and then buying powerful weapons from the rich western countries resulting in the balance of power shifting from western countries to Asia.

The long-term impact of all this is that as the power balance shifts towards Asia, the western countries become weak and also the Asian countries have also gained supremacy in supplying generic medicines to the Western countries which are several times cheaper than those made in the western countries. In times of pandemic the requirements of the medicines become huge resulting in the western countries becoming heavily depend on the Asian countries to fulfil their requirements.

Coming back to World War I, which happened between the years 1914-1918, resulted in 20 million people being killed from all over the World. When those people returned from the war-ravaged countries, they brought disease with the, which they inherited from the jungles, which lead to the great pandemic of the 1920s in which several more million people died.

The beginning of war starts with the start of nationalism, where the political leader uses the term "I want my country to be the greatest on Earth", this slogan has a very big effect on the mindset of the public in that country, the same situation was used by Osama Bin Laden and the same slogan is used by big political leaders in Asia and Western countries and the same slogan was used by Hitler in Germany and also during World War I & II.

Whenever such situation's come war is inevitable as without war those leaders cannot become supreme leaders of the world. These leaders want the public in their country to worship them as Gods and also want people of other countries to recognize them as Gods, which is a form of cyko phobia. They rake up likes and supporters on social media by spending money to create millions of fake supporters, which act as support to convince those who are not part of this madness.

The cause of world wars was due to Nationalism and increase in military power of the nations at that time. A similar situation exists today, where many nations have become too powerful for their own good, due to increase in military power and collection of weapons like museums financed through taxing the public. So the entire thing is free of cost for the nations.

After a country becomes more powerful than the rest of the countries, it is much like an Olympic race; the leader of that country automatically becomes a powerful figure compared to other political leaders, much like an Olympic player getting more than one gold medal. This means he becomes more popular in other countries as well. Another method of a leader becoming popular is that he starts buying weapons in large quantities for the purpose of war citing nationalism and expansion and national security and uses it to bolster his image internationally. It is like a celebratory that breaks lot of records, earns lot of money paid by advertising companies due to his huge popularity in breaking records in sports games.

The leader then tries to create an artificial conflict at the border with another country, and accuses that country more powerful than him of aggression. He then asks support of other powerful countries to help him, since his country is small. The other powerful countries chip in to help in form of free armies, and alliances are formed to fight the powerful enemy. Most of the other powerful countries also have a grudge against those powerful countries, resulting in mutual benefit, even for a cause which was not genuine in the first place but a trick by a smaller country to make the big countries fight each other.

This has been happening time and again and some countries have small land areas but are able to sit in equality with big countries due to their huge population, which capitalist economies like the United States think are a big market for their products and technologies. So while some countries are powerful due to large land mass, those countries with huge population are equally powerful due to a large population, which makes everyone bow to them. Although, the large population is detrimental for the countries themselves as well as for the capitalist countries, as most of the jobs in capitalist countries are overtaken by the cheap labour from those countries with those huge populations.

The World War I happened due to Nationalism and expansion of military power and a small country like Austria attacking to take over Serbia in alliance with Hungary. Serbia tied up with Russia to defend itself and different countries ended up forming alliances in the process leading to a World War I.

Similar situation exists in Tibet, which is also almost as barren and inhospitable as Serbia with low oxygen and lot of greenery and nature. Serbia has more ice which is needed for Earth to survive. Now India had attacked Tibet in the past in the 1800s taking over some territory. At that time, a king from Punjab province of disintegrated India partly under British and Muslim control and partly under some Hindu kings, tried to take over Tibetan territory, adjacent to India. China hardly had any border with India in those times. Tibet asked the help of China to ward off the attack and some Tibetan territory also went into hands of the Punjab king from India. There were several attempts later on also.

During independence in 1947, the British cleverly handed over Chinese and Tibetan lands to India, so they would forever remain in conflict and till today the situation exists with neither side ready to forego the occupied lands. Due to huge population, India requires more land and that land is only available with Tibet which has a low population like Serbia. So India wants to make Tibet independent, and wants to take over more Tibetan land than it was given by the British and the one it won in the India-China war in the 1960s. It has the support of the United States to overtake Tibet, like Austria-Hungary wanted to take over Serbia for its land mass.

Israelis were killed by Germany, and did not have their own land mass. They were given refuge by the Palestine people also called the Arabs. As Israeli population expanded, they found the land insufficient, for their needs and started pushing out the Arabs in the process leading to regular conflicts. The same situation exists in Kashmir, where 90 % of the population is Muslim. The British ignored the demand of Pakistan and gave the land to India, resulting in permanent enmity between the two nations. For India it is prestige issue, they cannot give Kashmir independence at any cost even if it means spending billions of dollars of taxpayers' money to keep Kashmir as Indian public is not in favor of making Kashmir independent. Even after Kashmir being part of India, the minority Kashmiri Hindu pundits who are very rich are not returning to Kashmir and instead joined posh government jobs, controlling the Indian government and fulfilling their agenda of hate by controlling the Indian military power and focusing entire money and attention on Kashmir, even after Kashmir is part of India.

Indian people want Kashmir even after 99% Indians never go to Kashmir, and it takes away major part of Indian taxes even after its contribution to India's GDP is insignificant. The northern parts of India having Chinese and Tibetan people like Mizoram, Manipur, Assam, Arunachal Pradesh, Meghalaya, Tripura and Sikkim are culturally different, being Chinese and Tibetan, and of different skins but still Indian resources and army is more focused on defending these occupied lands resulting in a 2400 km of border to defend with several neighbouring countries. This has resulted in these barren, icy and cold lands, becoming strategically important, require 24 hours patrolling which would not have normally required had these lands been under their actual countries and with actual people.

Gujarat and Rajasthan two states of India have much longer bordered with Pakistan but there is hardly any presence of any army between the two countries at this border, even after the entire border is porous. But those other states which have much smaller borders with Pakistan are having more military on both sides with regular intrusions by terrorists. This is because drugs and money enter through these borders, go to Mumbai, and from there go to Western countries for sale.

India spends more money on retaining these lands given by the British than on its own people in the form of maintaining more military and in the result having more conflicts with its neighbours. Obviously, the conflicts will never end as these people are not Indian Hindus in the first place and have all of their relatives and ancestors in China and Tibet. Anyone speaking against this in India automatically becomes anti-nationalist. China and Tibet want their lands back and India cannot give them back as it would mean loss of face and prestige, so the conflict will someday turn into a war. Either India, would want more of Chinese, and Tibetan lands or the Chinese and Tibet people would want their lands back, which were given by the British to India.

Similar situation exists in lands occupied by the United Stated from Mexico but it is on lesser degree as most of the culture of both these countries match. When Austria tried to take over Serbia, Russia came to the defence. A Serbian, which was later labelled as terrorist, killed Archduke Franz Ferdinand, who was the heir apparent to Austria, leading to World War I, with Austria-Hungary declaring war on Serbia. As a result, Russia came to the defence of Serbia and Germany came to the support of Austria. France came to the defence of Russia, resulting in Germany attacking France in repulsion, using Belgium. Similar to when India can only attack

China through Nepal. After Germany used Belgium to attack France, Britain had to join in to defend France.

The resulting alliance was Austria-Hungary and Germany on one side.

The opposite alliance was France, Russia, Serbia, Belgium, and Britain, with the United States, Italy and Japan joining them later.

All the countries including Britain, Russia and Germany had build up huge militaries during that time. Like Nepal, Belgium was a neutral country and similar to how Nepal is sandwiched between India and China, Belgium was also sandwiched between Germany and France, who was an ally of Russia at that time.

In an India China war which may take place in the near future, India will attack China through Nepal if it attacks first and in case of China, they will attack from Ladakh and Bhutan and Tibet. Different countries will tie up depending on their financial and military interests when the actual war takes place. Russia will have to defend Tibet and China, even after it is friends with India, as the United States is totally in favour of supporting India, even after it has more financial investments in China. Some loss is acceptable to reduce dominance of China in world economy.

India wants to become superpower but does not qualify due to low land area and more population than the land it has at present and its population increases faster than its land area. Even after knowing this reality, the United States has no choice but to support India and even the European countries are strongly in favour of supporting India for the same reasons.

Both China and India dominate the world with cheap medicines called generic medicines which are copied from the Western countries. Both started at the same time, China supplies the cheap raw materials to India, and India packs them into finished medicines and sells them to the Western world. At present one third of all medicines in the Western countries are from India supplied through China as Western countries do not want to buy medicines from China, so India acts as a broker earning billions in the process. Chinese and Indians are therefore, both friends and enemies or we can say competitors to earn money from the western countries, who have money to buy but have costly labour and strict environmental laws preventing them from manufacturing the essential medicines, which result in generation of polluted waste.

They are selling the manufacturing technology for the medicines to China, who sells the raw materials to India, and since the packing of raw materials to finished products does not require technology, the finished products end up in the western world as India is a friendly nation of western countries. India and China have no pollution worries as the governments of their countries take care of it and bribes make it easy for industries to continue running polluted factories.

Availability of cheap medicines and vaccines has not reduced diseases as these cheap medicines create more diseases and side effects, resulting in more business for them both in domestic as well as international markets. Both India and China now have huge pharmacy companies and biological labs doing research on various types of viruses which can provide more business in form of vaccines and businesses. Everything is smoothly interrelated.

China is a communist country so is Russia, Cuba, Lao, Nepal and Vietnam. While the United States, almost all European countries except Russia, India are democratic countries. Types of governments in both communist countries and democratic countries is same including collecting taxes, employees and running governments almost 99% of the functions are same including the parliaments system of governance. The only difference is the alliances of each country, much like World War I situations. It is you to judge who is right and who is wrong.

One is left aligned, the other is right aligned like our hands are left and right, and the only common thing is all are part of the United Nations. Some people think that the United Nations are part of a new world order, but it was never part of that and will never be one. I will discuss this in brief only and the UN is a neutral body like the WHO – World health organization and the International Court of justice and some other institutions, which I will explain at a later period of time, when it will be required.

Countries can never be together, because of business interest. Wealth is never there and global trade helps to create virtual wealth and growth of GDP, although the actual population always remains poor no matter how much you trade, as there is a limit to one can trade goods and services. The more the trade, the more trade barriers have to be made and more taxes, with one cheating country tries to earn more money by taxing the goods and services to earn more income after it builds up a large amount of money through intangible goods such as software, software services and supplying cheap labour. Since this involves very less sale of actual physical goods it becomes an advantage over countries that have large land mass and supply physical goods. The country supplying services and also charging tax on services always benefits in the long term as its foreign currency reserves go on increasing and from services it buys all computer, laptops, communication equipment's, weapons etc. while its people work in other countries stealing their employments and that country taxes the other country as well as taxes its own people working in those countries gets double income in taxes as well as valuable foreign exchange.

It is also able to increase its reserves by manipulating its own currency up and down as it has the required foreign reserves much like that done in options trading increasing its foreign reserves by 4-5 % every year buying when the foreign currency is low and selling and buying back its own currency in open market when the dollar become high, without providing actual goods and services. These types of activities are financial wars, which are hard to catch and the cheating country often a poor third world country continues to loot the rich countries in this way and manages to buy goods with the same money which would not have been honestly possible, due to income discrepancy.

Political leaders have power in their hands which goes on increasing with every new law which is passed; in addition they have control to the spending on all the revenues made by the country and also have a hold on the public through elections creating a very strong support base.

When we created a democratic system, our purpose was never to make political leaders as Gods or let alone allow them to become supreme leaders or have millions of followers.; but in the process some leaders went out of the way to grant themselves extra virtual powers, which the public though was real powers, to try to be permanent, use the public money to increase their supporter bases by transferring public money to their supporters.

They benefitted big rich businessmen who financed their rise to power, and on the opposite side spend the public money on the poor people distributing them pennies, which was a huge bonus for those who had nothing. So the poor got bought cheaply for pennies or a bottle of booze for which they never had the money to purchase anyway in their entire lifetime.

Natural human tendency then is that these politicians become Gods for them as he is the first one to distribute pennies, which according to him even God did not give him in his entire lifetime on Earth. So that politician is much more valuable to be worshipped than God.

The Greeks, Egyptians, Romans, Mesopotamians, Hindus did try to make a New World Order. The ones who partially succeeded were the people from the Lost City of the Atlantic. They were the closest ones to have implemented the New World Order.

If I call the times when Roman's, Egyptians, Greeks, Hindus as behind in technology and the people as too illiterate to implement the New World Order it would partly be right and wrong. At that time knowledge was restricted to a few selected people under the royalty and the lords. The lords controlled the money, ministers ran the administration and knowledge was in hands of a few people who only transferred to the ruling head.

That is why expansion was limited, but as the knowledge spread to the common people it became a cause for conflict, more power and more wars resulting in destruction. This happened every time with the Roman's becoming more powerful, and also the Hindus, Greeks and Egyptians.

Because we cannot study so much history, we can infer same situations existed in those times, they had trade, business, GDP, growth, make unique items and sold to each other, made armies and created powerful economies and military power from business and trade and thus we know their downfall and destruction.

The leftover part is World War II which we will discuss now. In World War I, some parts of Serbia were under rule of Austria and when a freedom fighter killed one of the top leaders of Austria, it attacked Serbia resulting in the War and countries taking sides. World War I resulted in Germany becoming a republic in 1918 and many of the military powers ceased to exist which included Britain and Russia and there was also a revolution in Russia. William II was the Emperor of Germany at time of World War I. Most people world over would think it was Hitler at the time of World War I without going into the details. William II had very less hold over his military generals who had big war aims even after Germany lost in World

War I and the Emperor was forced to seek refuge in the Netherlands in 1918, after Germany lost the war and stayed there till his death in 1941. The military generals and the political leadership refused a compromise or peace with the allies forcing him to abdicate the throne.

This is how Germany went into the hands of military generals after World War I. All this you will not find on history books and in information on the internet, except the dates which are common, other things are looked at differently. World War I created two powerful military alliances and further set the seeds for World War II in 1939.

Democratic nations were established after World War I and most of the imperialistic powers ruled by kings and queens converted to democracy form of government which we see today. Many western nations even had parliaments and chancellors before, in addition to kings and queens. A League of Nations was established to sort our differences between the fighting nations. Due to abdication of the Emperor of Germany, William II to the Netherlands, Germany came in the hands of the military generals who spread the idea of Nationalism, which we saw in Afghanistan and now we see it in Hindus in India today. Hitler preached Germany as a superior race and promised more land for German people much like the Hindus want back Pakistan and Afghanistan, which they believe was an earlier part of India during the Mahabharata and also believe Kashmir was a Hindu kingdom.

Similar revolution also took place in Italy promoted by Mussolini, who was also a Dictator, at almost the same time, first it starting in Italy, then moving on to Germany. All these dictators, whether in Asia, Europe or elsewhere promote the same hate and nationalism and talk of re-occupying lands which may or may not have been in those countries in the past. This happens when such countries become powerful after doing international trade and business and building up a huge number of foreign reserves to manage any large scale reserves, a huge military as well as lots of arms and ammunitions.

Hitler was leader of the Nazi party, and during time of the great recession, used racism, hate and nationalism to rise to power and was equally supported by the military in Germany. Hitler became Chancellor in 1933, using a mix of racism, nationalism, superiority of the German race to rise to power and Osama Bin Laden used the same methods to incite Muslims. Hindu leaders also use the same methods to rise to power and use the German swastika symbol, nationalism, hate against Muslims and fascism. This hate is inbuilt in the public in all the nations and can be en-cashed anytime. Some country has occupied the other country in the past and many people try to restore things which are now impossible today.

Most of these are half educated people who have interpreted history in the wrong way, or the leaders glorify their country being great at some centuries before in the past, which works wonders in spreading hate and racism. Japan also followed a similar path calling the Japanese superior and tried to incite a conflict with China in the 1930s the same time as Italy and Germany. The Japanese occupied some of the Chinese ports and declared a part of Chinese lands independent supporting the rebels in 1931. Hitler from Germany and Mussolini from Italy had the same views on nationalism and became natural friends and tied up together much like Trump tided up with his Asian counterparts who were also nationalists wanting to break China. A series of small wars took place supported by Germany and Italy, in the 1930s as an experiment which would further lead to large scale occupation of other countries. These were financing the Spanish revolt and an Ethiopian war in 1935 by occupying Ethiopia by Hitler.

The countries with similar views used nationalism, racism, fascism and expansion which included Japan, Germany and Italy joined together to form a military coalition from 1936 to 1937. Hitler occupied Austria in 1938, got support of Mussolini and called it an internal affair of Germany which was accepted by Britain and France, much like Kashmir is called an internal affair of India. He then set his eyes on Czechoslovakia, which has 3-4 million Germans on its Western border and occupied it through a settlement with Czechoslovakia, helped by Britain, on the assurance that Hitler would not take over more lands of Czechoslovakia. But breaking his assurance, Hitler took over Czechoslovakia in 1939 and then set eyes on Poland, which was under protection of France.

Another Dictator had also taken birth in Russia who was Stalin, almost at the same time. Hitler made a pact with Stalin to prevent Russia from interfering in 1939, by sharing Poland which was occupied by Germany in 1939, and then proceeded to occupy

Finland, Romania, and Estonia, Latvia which also Hitler shared jointly with Russia.

As before, also China was weak in the 1920s and Japan set its eyes on China and occupied most part of it and invaded China in 1937 before that occupying several parts of China slowly, before that it had taken over Korea in 1905 and was an imperialistic power. Japan had to withdraw after its aggression was opposed by the League of Nations.

Germany, Japan and Italy became partners with Germany and Japan doing the expansion occupying countries with weak military power and looting, raping and arson, between 1939, to 1945, which is called as World War II. One of the reasons for this was these countries were heavily in debts after World War I and suffering the great depression of their economies. They shared the spoils with the other countries.

After, becoming more and more powerful through war and occupying other countries, Japan decided to attack the United States in Pearl Harbor, its largest naval base, in 1941 and the results are known to everyone, where the Japanese bombed it heavily, destroyed it and left. This angered the Americans, who declared war on Japan. Japan was supported by Hitler, who also declared war against the United States.

In all in the World War II, 100 million people took part in the war and the end result was the defeat of Germany and Japan, which happened after the United States entered the war after attack by Japan on Pearl Harbor in 1941. The rest is history and you can find all the other information on the internet itself without having to repeat it all over here.

CHAPTER FIVE
Taxation and Identity cards

People switch from New World Order to Old World Order when taxes become high enough that they are impossible to pay them, they start running up debts and everything becomes upside down. They have luxury houses, gadgets, good education, all types of luxuries but end up with a huge load of debt in the process as everything they were given to use cars, mobile phones, digital payments, transactions, identity cards, bank accounts, stock trading, costly apartments bough when income was high, credit cards, crypto currency sucks all the money they have and almost everyone is in debt.

Now people are no longer interested in those luxury goods and want to return back to zero just want food and water to survive, they even don't want education and political leaders and cannot even afford a government which has more expenses and employees then the work it does. The government is working more like a multinational company doing business of collecting money through taxes, selling government lands, government owned companies, offering leases, collecting toll taxes for the roads it builds which was earlier constructed from the central tax collection. The government enters almost all types of businesses in this process getting free money in the form of taxes, selling national companies to other countries to get more money and build up reserves and uses the money to buy weapons, upgrade military, do technology research, space exploration, make missiles, stock weapons of mass destruction as defense, built a huge military and do all kinds of wring things, all financed for free through taxes.

In each of these cases to expand Technology, knowledge, military and increase the employee base of the government, resulted in taxing more and more people and taxing unlimited types of activities also called "chungi" which was an earlier form of toll tax in one of those old civilizations.

So the Roman, Greek, Hindu, Egyptian, Mesopotamian ,are New World Order and not the World order made by God. To repeat the Old World Order made by us is nature in all its natural forms –

Trees, animals, oceans, water kingdom of fishes and other speeches, air kingdom of birds and the mountains, valleys, rivers, ponds, land masses, islands and much more which you already know and have seen all these in your surroundings or visited some which are not there near you in the form of tourist places.

All the New World Order got destroyed from time to time because of taxation and like inflation taxes increase with time, as taxes increase so doe's inflation. Inflation is totally dependent on taxes. The price of all goods and services increase, only due to taxes. When taxes are reduced price of goods automatically come down. Sometimes governments cleverly reduce taxes for some goods and parallels increase the prices for other goods and services to collect more revenue, to avoid the displeasure of the public and also collect more revenues in the process.

The public gets fooled several times every year in this process, and it has always been a successful strategy with one part of public happy and the other dissatisfied resulting in division of the public who benefitted from the one who lost ending up paying more taxes. This is called a divide and rule policy.

As New World Order expands, it taxes more and more, finds new ways of generating taxes, first finances terrorism, then creates security. The New World Order asks for identity proofs, creates business when people go to make the national identity cards, and offers food coupons which is also a business, employs people to check identity cards, asks for employee verification, and creates business for making employee identification cards and identification equipment.

Surprisingly, none of the countries create voter identity cards or verify voter identity neither have the means to cross check voting or prevent fake voting. If the governments were really interested, voter identity is the main identity which will make everything smooth and honest. While national identity cards and employee cards in addition to driving licenses, insurance cards, country passports and similar documents are unique but voter identity cards are not and people have multiple of them after shifting from one state to another due to genuine reasons and many are forged and duplicates also.

There is another business where once you are forced to make those cards, then whose who cannot obtain them due to financial difficulty or lack of proper documents forge them as they are unable to survive without those documents. Then people are employed to arrest those who are not having the documents, arrested for trying to forge documents and all this seems right people should be arrested for forgery.

But here is the catch, people start employing lawyers, after getting caught means more business for lawyers and courts, then some pay bribes after getting caught and so on with endless possibilities. So did the identity cards benefit people are created more problems than solutions.

Also, if the identity cards are so important why the government employees are not having them where is it more important. In some countries where attendance is not necessary, government employees have been found working at two or more jobs not even attending offices and even sending other people to attend work. There those rules of identity verification do not apply.

Identities are being asked only at places where actually there is no requirement of it at all. When millions of people have those identity cards, then the checking of identity cards becomes cumbersome and the security people become in excess and tiredness takes place at airports, public places and entrances of work locations. Then those identity cards become useless after that demand comes for making another new form of identity like Tax ID cards, then there are insurance cards, food cards, travel cards, toll tax cards, and the list is endless.

The uneducated which are 80% of the world population or more then start to either steal cards of genuine people, since they lose source of income generation as they are unable to make those cards. They then start doing crimes using stolen or forged cards which are much easier than going through the documentation for making them and paying bribes in addition to having genuine documents.

CHAPTER SIX

Crime generation through New World Order and Identity cards

Identity cards are also the first forms of the New World Order and the start of new types of crimes other than rape, murder and theft that is why we are devoting so much time to them. Also, they are contributing to employing new security people in unlimited quantity resulting in us paying more and more taxes and buying unwanted security equipment's which were not required earlier and 24 -hour monitoring of shops, offices, roads, radar monitoring and so on.

When a New World Order is implemented, crimes eventually take place and crimes and saturation of New World Order is almost simultaneous. One of the forms of crime generation through a New World Order, which I explained is through the requirements of identity cards for people on the planet and the identity cards being specific to each region, state or country.

God allowed us to be born on Earth without an identity card; he did not feel it necessary to send an identity card along with our birth. It was not thought of as necessary. Then what made them necessary. Some countries collected taxes in the starting of the New World Order as a requirement for giving free or concession grains to the poor and needy. To only allow the poor and the needy to get these items required them to have ration cards and the rich could not make those ration cards if their income was above a certain level.

Also, it was below dignity for rich people to have ration cards and relatives and friends would make fun of them if they did make them and went to the ration shops as people would make fun of them behind their backs. But when inflation increased as it does, due to taxation, the rich no longer felt insulted in using grains from ration shops and even managed to make the ration cards by paying bribes.

The governments soon made the ration cards as identification proofs resulting in them becoming compulsory for everyone alike be it the rich or the poor. People now made forget and duplicate ration cards to get more concessional food as buying outside food was costly.

So crime generation automatically took place, first with ration cards it was ok, but after taxing the price of open market items increased, resulting in the rich or the middle rich people also requiring food cards which were not needed earlier. To manage the food cards and distribution, the government needed to employ more people, corruption started in buying and distribution of ration and even the ration shops sold the left-over grains in open market secretly.

Now the people had millions of such cards real, fake and duplicate ones, so the government said the old ration cards are now obsolete and the public will have to make new ones as it is difficult to check which is real and which is fake as entire process of making the cards was manual and the information was only in handwritten registers at several thousand government offices located all over the country making verification difficult.

To implement the new system required more money so new taxes on say fuels like petrol; diesel and home gas was raised in addition to taxes on other household goods and some of the services. The salaries of government employees were also raised to cope with the extra work.

Soon, duplicates and fakes of ration cards also became common and almost everyone had those ration cards as they were the only form of identification of making new bank accounts, driving licenses, purchasing vehicles, opening new businesses, buying property etc. Here also the records were manual and then the government wanted to collect all the data at one source.

Again, a new business started of collecting the different records, which were in hundreds of millions, so came the manual and electronic typewriters to make the records, and then came the computer which stored those records.

To purchase computers, power supplies, they needed more taxes, and then came printers, storage devices and the internet to transfer the data and so on. This resulted in more and more taxes. As technology increased the military also wanted those gadgets resulting in more taxes to pay for them. Then comes the requirement for the software to run those systems, store data and transfer it from one place to another.

The computers, printers, and software found multiple uses in military, industry, education, science, space technology, and military aircrafts and for building weapons of mass destruction and several other gadgets for mobile communication.

This knowledge was exclusive to a few countries and soon the word spread and other countries started spying and stealing those technologies. Some stole them by buying off people and then to prevent stealing copyright laws came, then to implement they required security and tie up with countries where those gadget technologies or software was copied and made. Again, addition of crime took place resulting in employing more security people and buying more security gadgets and developing new security gadgets.

To make new technology public had to work and pay, and to catch the thief's also public had to pay additional taxes. This is how it has been going on till today, public pays for every new technology through taxes and we think it is made free.

We pay to make and research for the new technology and we also pay to buy the gadgets made from our own money, then we also pay recurring payments for using those technologies and again for upgrades and replacements and repairs.

Everything is related to only identity cards, every technology was made for making identity cards, verifying identity cards and using identity cards. Every technology which will be made in the future will be made for identification, re-identification and changing old identity cards and making new ones. This is the only activity the New World Order does and, in the results, employs more government employees, more military personnel, buying new weapons and making weapons of mass destruction.

Nobody in the world till today till the time of writing this book ever realized that one identity card has been fooling the world all the time and every time.

Was   this   needed   in   the   first   place?

CHAPTER SEVEN
Taxation and the Barter System

Before Taxation even existed we had the Barter system of exchanging and paying for the goods and services. This worked across several kingdoms within the countries and also outside the kingdoms between the people. Taxation came much later.

When countries did not exist which we refer to the Old World Order, people started making goods from stones, objects from trees and started to learn to grow plants for food. It is a long story, but it has to be told, so we will cover it entirely in some other part of this book. Some of it is taught in books and some of it may be there in reference books and some other information in encyclopedias and I don't have time to read so many books and will pass on as God tells them to me or through what I read earlier or through Artificial Intelligence the new Technology buzz word. Artificial intelligence is not new and I will also tell how God invented Artificial Intelligence in the first place and how it is being reused.

The purpose of Taxation has always been there and there is no deny to the fact that it has been there in the Old World Order as well as the New World Order. Only the meaning of Taxation has changed over the time. It will still be there for times immortal or till mankind survives if it does.

Taxation will also go ways in extreme natural calamities like earthquakes, floods, nuclear wars, mass destruction, famines wiping out most part of humanity and other calamities like pandemics. This is what we call regeneration and Taxation also goes down in recession.

First, we will discuss how Taxation became a necessity and why its graph always goes up and never goes down unless there is an extreme natural calamity, pandemic, war or recession.

We had taxes at the time of Kings, before that we had a barter system since money was not there in circulation. So the Barter system was used for exchange of goods, and services during ancient times.

Before explaining the Taxation and the Barter system one has to go through the prehistoric times when we made the entire planet.

CHAPTER EIGHT

Prehistoric times to present time

As explained earlier in one of my books ours is a Type 7 planet, which means life can survive on this planet due to the ideal nature of distance from the Sun, ability to hold water in liquid form and ability to have an atmosphere, optimum gravity and several other factors which we have not find it possible on other planets.

When we made humans and other animals and the different species which you now call as natural evolution, we did not make them permanent and there was no reproduction. Where we made them and how we made them will not be discussed or told to you, and you may guess yourself with Darwin's theory of evolution or monkeys converting themselves to human beings leaving rest of the monkey race behind to fend for themselves.

After the planet was created which required a lot of efforts and likewise we had millions of workers working simultaneously, researching and upgrading the living beings. Initially we made the entire planet from oceans, rivers, mountains, plants, trees, beautifying them and so one as much as we could.

After our task of creating the nature was completed which included making the clouds, seasons, putting water into oceans etc. we started on the process of creating nature and greenery.

The living beings came later much after to live on this vast and empty planet. We made temporary living beings which did not have reproduction capacity to reproduce their offspring's, so every time they died, we had to make new ones and bring them to the planet and we also had to supply them food which lasted only a few days and it was not practical since travel was difficult.

I have skipped some important parts here which cannot be disclosed as of now. Since replacing the living beings and plants was cumbersome, we made seeds for plants and developed reproduction for the living beings, which eased our requirements to transport plants and animals to the planet every time.

Naturally, all of them were ignorant and illiterate and as explained by your scientists, who they call the natural theory of evolution, you learned to live, grow, become more knowledgeable and rear animals and grow plants and do more activities.

For you this is theory of evolution and for God who made it is its Artificial Intelligence. Since we are discussing the Old and New World Order, the Bible, Testament, Koran, Vedas and other holy books are the first teachings made by us when you learned to read and write.

The Human mind took 2000-10,000 years to develop its artificial intelligence to make Robots, planes, cars, mobile phones and other technologies which are called theory of evolution. But surprisingly when making Robots, cars, mobile phones, 3G, 4G, 5G and upgrading those technologies does not come under any theory of evolution of non-living things which move.

If bacteria evolved into living organisms, as scientists say, then why cannot we say that cars, mobile phones, internet and other technologies have evolved themselves?

If Humans are Gods for mobiles, robots, and other gadgets as they made them so there is a God who made the humans and other living beings that is why you go to holy places to worship him.

The prehistoric times were bad, we were still in evolution and did not even know anything and started with polishing rocks, making splinted edges out of them and sharp enough to hunt animals, then came the bows and arrows we learnt to make from wood, then the clothes from the leaves, and fibers of plants, then houses from the leaves, trunks and also the wooden houses came after that.

So we were not as intelligent then as we are today and it took us centuries to become so intelligent and it is all through education and preservation of history and science. Things which we discovered in the past were stored for future generations to read and carry over much like we carry ancient history, this is how technology expanded. Rest is for you to figure out using your artificial intelligence. This same artificial intelligence we are trying to use in software and also in robots, automatic cars and industrial machinery, trying to make them inorganic human beings eliminating the organic human beings slowly.

Someday, we may no longer have the human race as the robots, cars and industrial equipment's become intelligent enough to eliminate humanity, as they have no difficulty in travelling in space, have no breathing problems and have no issues living in hot, cold and extreme climatic conditions such as floods, famines and earthquakes.

This is the speed with which artificial intelligence is taking over our lives.

Role of Values, Ideologies, and Soft Power

Values, ideologies, and soft power play a significant role in shaping the new world order. They influence international relations by shaping the perceptions, behaviours, and alliances of nations.

1. Cultural Exchanges: Cultural exchanges, including arts, literature, music, and education, facilitate mutual understanding and foster goodwill among nations. Cultural diplomacy and people-to-people connections contribute to building trust and bridging cultural gaps.

2. Human Rights; Human rights principles, such as individual freedoms, equality, and the rule of law, have become global norms. Nations that uphold these values often have more positive international reputations. Violations of human rights can lead to diplomatic and economic consequences.

3. Democratic Ideals; Democratic ideals, including free and fair elections, representative governance, and respect for civil liberties, are valued by many nations and supported by international organizations. Democracies often cooperate more closely with one another and share common values.

4. Soft Power: Soft power, a concept coined by Joseph Nye, refers to a nation's ability to influence others through attraction and persuasion rather than coercion or force. Soft power sources include culture, political values, foreign policies, and diplomatic efforts. It can be a potent tool in shaping international relations.

Impact on International Relations

1. Cultural Diplomacy: Cultural diplomacy and exchanges promote cross-cultural understanding, fostering positive international relations and reducing misunderstandings and stereotypes.

2. Human Rights; Nations that prioritize human rights and align their foreign policies accordingly often build stronger alliances and partnerships based on shared values.

3. Democratic Thinking: Democracies tend to cooperate more closely, forming alliances like NATO, and share common diplomatic goals, such as promoting democracy and human rights worldwide.

Influence of Different Worldviews and Political Systems

1. Authoritarian Systems: Authoritarian states may prioritize stability and control over human rights and democratic values. They often engage in strategic partnerships based on economic interests rather than shared political values.

2. Liberal Democracies: Liberal democracies often seek alliances with like-minded nations that share their political values and institutions. They promote democracy and human rights in their foreign policies.

3. Mixed Systems: Some nations have mixed political systems, combining elements of both authoritarianism and democracy. Their behaviour in international relations may be influenced by a range of factors.

4. Non-State Actors: Non-state actors, including multinational corporations, civil society organizations, and transnational networks, also play a role in shaping international relations. They can promote values and ideals independently of states.

Values, ideologies, and soft power are integral components of the new world order. They influence state behaviour, shape international alliances, and impact global perceptions of nations. The alignment or clash of these values and ideologies plays a pivotal role in determining the dynamics of international relations in the 21st century.

CHAPTER NINE
Taxation in modern times

Taxation today has acquired entirely different meanings; it is called fast development and governments look for all goods and services which presently have no tax but involve money exchange. Something you are buying or selling using money which has previously not been included in the tax net.

Eating food, no tax, attack the food sellers and tax them. Labor services not taxed, people getting salary or money tax the contractor, transport not taxed make it applicable. Doctors, hospitals no longer classify as essential services tax them also. Medicines to be taxed too, part time jobs to be taxed, selling water, and oxygen tax them too.

Now there is no limit and the central bank is flush with money, prices of goods and services go on increasing, making it harder and harder, and a collapse is inevitable. The government doesn't want to stop as people ready to pay, standing outside the house, take it, take it says the public, tax everything. Father dies pay tax, mother dies pay tax, any relative or friend dies pay tax, everyone is ready to pay. The government promises more jobs to security people if it collects more taxes to safeguard its money, weapons, military and government employees as all of these increases with increased money collection through taxes.

More security is required because government is collecting more money than ever and all government buildings want security, all army areas want security to safeguard the weapons they bought, the ships and aircrafts they bought with the taxes. Security is required to prevent the unsatisfied people from attacking the government over the taxes.

The first purpose of taxes in the olden times and new ones was to provide road cleaning and clean all types of waste and supply water and sanitation. Slowly, building roads, dams, providing electricity, maintenance activities, paying for salary of the government employees, travel, government housing for employees, perks, maintaining an army, buying weapons, ships, missiles, ammunition, guns, computers, faxes, printers, building parliaments, municipal and state buildings and thousands of such things got added from time to time.

It never went down, except in Yugoslavia and some other countries where the agitations burnt down everything and in Iraq and some other places where the governments ceased to exist or in times of war.

Taxes never go down and the demands for new things for governments also never go down, so inflation which increases only due to taxation or in the event of a shortage always remains on top.

This is the New World Order which has always been there, but you have never seen it. Taxation has always been the New World Order which makes everyone afraid and dictates everything.

Interest is another virtual thing part of the New World Order which eats away everything we have and it is also a killer disease much like any diseases we have in our body. For some paying high interest rates it is like having diabetes and having to take insulin injections every month, never ending till you die. Some recover like a mild fever, if the loan amounts are small and can be paid off from existing income sources.

Interest is charged when government lends money to everyone including itself through banks, and the interest is income to the government. Since there is always a shortage of money, banks also accept deposits from the public in addition to borrowing money from the government. The banks pay an interest difference to the public or the government and the difference is the gross profit of the bank. Less the expenses give banks as net profit.

Developed countries have reduced interest and some of those countries even charge people for depositing money, but in third world countries the governments still charge heavy interest rates.

CHAPTER TEN

The Aliens

No one has seen aliens; even the videos are unclear, having only flashes of lights in them classified as alien aircrafts. One department of the government claims to have contact with the aliens doing research activities with them building new weapons, bombers, aircrafts and advanced gadgets but some other intelligence department within the same government does not even know about it even after several claims come up of aliens being present.

Presently, we are so advanced, that we can detect missiles, planes, any flying objects though radar and sophisticated surveillance equipment's which we have developed. We can even stop incoming missiles in the air and so on and detect intrusion of any types on the borders and satellites can see anywhere on the Earth.

Surprisingly, with all these surveillance systems, we have not been able to detect any alien aircraft or objects. Those seen are either flash of light, light balls, irregular light phenomena, falling objects, of some kind seen from a very large distance, and are very small to be identified as to what they are.

In some of the videos which they have claimed to have caught the aliens the body only shows human parts and none of them appear alien ones. The files are so secret that it seems more of being fabricated then real, and one gets to know the information only after the person holing the information dies, se we don't even know if that person had actually written the information. Police and intelligence agencies are not allowed to investigate or have access to the alien bodies and neither the scientific community has access to any alien items for research.

The supposed to be alien bodies appear to be children or human bodies mutilated to appear as aliens and injected with some sort of chemicals to enlarge their head and perform some sorts of experiments similar to the ones done in cloning to create super human beings or beings to have more intelligence or memory.

The bodies of the aliens are not powerful enough to even fight or live in inhospitable conditions on Earth, on their ships and have no protective suits. Neither the skulls, bones, nor other body parts are there in museums even after we have several Egyptian ones in museums which have bodies different from the ones, we have at present very tall and thin humans.

So many aircrafts are flying around protecting countries round the clock having all modern cameras are catching only faint and unclear pictures of aircrafts or drones which resemble the alien like aircrafts or toy aircrafts run remotely are being shown as alien aircrafts, making it some kind of a hoax.

When you read all of the classified documents which they have stored in different drawers, you will find that none of them are true at all and seem some kind of hoax to get the governments to spend money on research projects using the alien gimmick.

The political leader who is fighting the elections doesn't know it either even after being head of the government and he is still dependent on the public for becoming a head of state. Not only this are the aliens not giving him any orders of any kind or deciding his policies even after being so powerful.

All around the heads of states, in government buildings and everywhere there are security cameras and even after that aliens are not   detected.   Why?

CHAPTER ELEVEN

The secret evil and dark societies on Earth

Dark societies have always existed and acquired the new form of the dark web. It is not new and has always been real, a hidden world from the open one, we live in. Most politicians, rulers, top government officers, rich, wealthy, powerful people, celebrities, criminals, drug lords, mafia and other unlawful people are part of these secret societies.

Some evil societies operate legally and are registered as clubs and other forms and those who did not get permissions to register are illegal, but still run without any hindrances. These societies help to get that work done which is somewhat difficult or impossible to be done the normal way, and which is required for executing a business, contract, or doing a big transaction involving large amounts of money or permission from top authorities in a government and cannot be done due to the country's laws creating a hindrance.

This is only one example of that work and there are also other ones which include devil worship, drug parties, intermingling of the worst kinds imaginable, some of which now happen legally also, cults, other un recognized religions or lesser known, witches, who worship the demonic forces.

Some say the actual governments are run by these people and speak of some families which are wealthier than governments. Their names are never known to public and no law is applicable to them forever. Till now not even one head of state has been able to touch them or even see them or even know if they exist.

They even say these wealthy families have wealth in excess of 500 billion dollars and have influence on many countries and their leaders.

These evil societies even financed countries during the war when they were left almost with no money. The societies/families also finance the countries in times of need.

CHAPTER TWELVE
The real New World Order

The real New World order is one which will be run by the secret societies, in partnership with governments. So ultimately, it means the humans will operate simply as robots much like deer in the jungles, without any powers. Indirectly such systems do exist on an individual level where some unknown person becomes a politician, gets support from the secret cult societies, rises up to become a leader of the district, state or country.

He gets unknown findings from these cults which have rich and influential people and follows their agenda, tries to become a dictator or a global leader and impose his thinking in his own country as well as outside his country. So, a natural phenomenon comes which either destroys the country in which this dictator comes or results in this dictator creating wars and conflicts with its neighbors'.

We don't want the New World Order as it will be run by secret societies, there will be limits to freedom of speech and writing anything or criticizing will be an offense. People will have to live and work online; there will be restrictions on movement of people. All activities will be digitally stored and only rights of freedom will be granted to a selected few people who will be big businessmen, rich people and people close to the powerful politicians.

New World Order will also be boundary less means it will work across countries, which means all your personal information will be accessible to any investigating agency around the world including your face, fingerprints and genes information. Crypto currency may become the currency of the future and also many other things may happen where you will merely be a puppet.

All this has started to implement on a small scale, although it is very rapid, but appears small as it has to cover the entire population of the Earth and then will integrate into one big thing.

Some political leaders are even now trying to take over farm lands, which will result in food supply being totally controlled in the hands of a few individuals; this is also something like a New World Order.

Farmers also called peasants have always been left out of any New World Order implementations, and whenever, it was tried to be done, the Romans, Egyptians, Greeks and other civilizations, it led to their downfall.

The day they succeed in taking over farm lands, means we will no longer have control of our lives and livelihoods, as they have already taken over water and air even supplying oxygen today and existing of life will become very difficult for the majority of mankind irrespective of country and also costly to live.

But like any New World Order before that tried to enter this one will also be destroyed and how it will be done cannot be disclosed and can only be told by time and nature, who is the supreme owner of everything on the planet Earth as well as outside it.

It is also possible that those people are also part of the New World Order who was defeated in World War I & II and those associated with the old rules of the Kings and Queens who still hope of a comeback of the good old days. This also includes the ministers and royally below the kings and queens who actually controlled most of the power. Rest is for you to figure out as to what is actual truth.

CHAPTER THIRTEEN
God the Almighty Supreme Being

God is the Oldest World Order and over the time god has retained the World order even after several attempts to change the World order has been made by several types of entities.

When the planet was made, we ran under an automatic system, where first we allowed all types of freedom of movement, free air, water, food and free to live wherever we want. This holds true even today. We will advocate this freedom even after it has been changed by successive entities.

Some of the changes were done by God and some were done by those entities. In our Old World Order we had been successful in running the planet smoothly for thousands of years, but those Old World Orders have been slowly destroyed by new entities which now use inorganic elements such as Robots, planes, missiles, bombs, industrial revolution, capitalism, powerful militaries and border conflicts and wars as well as inter country trade to become rich and displace the delicate balance of the planet including building mass destructive nuclear and biological weapons to get ahead of each other.

This is a never-ending process which cannot be ended by us and it has to meet its own end. We have to take care of several things and when it does not work and the World does not obey the commandments of God then everything goes away, then there is no World order required neither the Old-World Order neither the New World Order which you are forcing on yourselves.

God accepts change as it happens naturally and you must have seen our old age people insist on following the old traditions and customs. While the new generation wants everything new and wants to discard old values and beliefs. So, the Old-World Order and New World Order are already known to you.

While God accepts the New World requirements, he does not accept the New World order. So mobile phones, computers, planes, vehicles and number of things are accepted as necessity but we do not accept changing age-old traditions and values. God also does not accept changing human minds and also displacing nature is not at all acceptable.

Our priority is to maintain the Old-World Order but the new generation will not accept it and is tired of the old traditions and values, so God does a reset in which everything becomes fresh and new. Then the new generation automatically understands the value of our old traditions and habits.

The Old-World Order means respecting parents, looking after them as they looked after us, respecting old traditions and values, following the old system of family management and preserving the nature, and the natural surroundings.

The survival of the Earth depends on preserving the Old-World Order which means if Old World Order is disturbed it will cause pollution, unlimited vehicles, unlimited roads, concrete multi-storied structures, use of unlimited water, carbon fuels, conflicts, military races, terrorism, fight for border lands and friction between countries for supremacy.

Although, some of these defects also existed in the past they will continue to do so in the future also, but when drastic changes take place, it will eventually lead to destruction of a major portion of mankind.

First of all, the Ozone layer is the lifeline of the planet, when I mentioned it many years back everyone repeats my story as his own. The Ozone layer protects the Earth from harmful radiations of the Sun enabling life to survive on Earth.

Excessive use of carbon fuels, vehicles, industrial activity and movement of millions of people to and from work to mention only a few of these activities leads to depletion of the Ozone layer which will then eventually end all life on Earth.

Man has been known to survive many tough situations and when destruction came in the past hundreds of years ago, he still survived in many ways which meant going to live in caves, digging underground structures, living on trees, climbing mountains to survive natural calamities and may have to do the same in future natural and un natural calamities and even going to the North and South poles to live.

CHAPTER FOURTEEN
Conclusion

Transition from the Old to the New World Order

The transition from the old-world order, characterized by Western dominance, to the new world order is a significant global transformation. Key factors driving this shift include the rise of China, the resurgence of Russia, and the changing role of the United States. The old-world order's power structures, shaped by Western powers, are giving way to a more multipolar distribution of power, where multiple actors wield influence on the global stage.

This transition is marked by

Rise of China: China's economic ascendancy, global trade initiatives like the Belt and Road Initiative, diplomatic influence, and military modernization challenge the traditional Western-dominated order.

Resurgence of Russia: Russia, under Putin's leadership, has pursued a more assertive foreign policy, influenced its former Soviet states and expanded its energy dominance.

Changing Role of the United States: The United States, while still a global superpower, faces relative decline, evolving foreign policy priorities, and shifts in international alliances and commitments.

Uncertainties and Complexities in the Evolving Global Landscape

The transition to the new world order introduces uncertainties and complexities

Geopolitical Implications: The multipolar world is characterized by shifting alliances, competition, and potential conflicts. The South China Sea, Ukraine, and the Taiwan Strait are examples of geopolitical flashpoints.

Global Challenges: Issues like climate change, cybersecurity, and pandemics transcend borders, necessitating international cooperation. However, differences in national interests and sovereignty concerns complicate effective collaboration.

Technological Advancements: Rapid technological advancements, including AI and cybersecurity, present both opportunities and threats. They reshape global power dynamics and challenge traditional concepts of warfare.

Future Developments, Challenges, and Opportunities

The future of the new world order will be influenced by:

Economic Shifts: Economic dynamics will continue to evolve as nations compete for technological leadership, access to resources, and economic growth.

Geopolitical Tensions: Tensions will persist in areas of territorial disputes, cybersecurity, and great-power competition. Diplomacy, conflict resolution, and cooperation will shape international relations.

Environmental Concerns: Climate change will drive global action, with opportunities for green technology, renewable energy, and sustainable development.

Values and Ideology: The role of values, ideologies, and soft power will influence state behaviour and global alliances, impacting international relations.

Encouraging Further Research and Discussion

The complexities and uncertainties of the evolving global landscape require continued research and discussion. Scholars, policymakers, and global citizens must engage in meaningful dialogue to address these critical global issues. International cooperation, diplomacy, and multilateralism will be essential in navigating the challenges and opportunities of the new world order.

Did you love *The Old and New World Order*? Then you should read
Secrets of Mount Kailash, Bermuda Triangle and the Lost City of Atlantis by Jagdish Arora!

The book goes into the details on the mysteries surrounding Mount Kailash, Bermuda Triangle, and the Lost City of Atlantis. It is also a good book to read for people who like to travel to unknown and mysterious places in the mountains and jungles.

'Secrets of Mount Kailash, Bermuda Triangle, and the Lost City of Atlantis' invites you to explore the world's most intriguing mysteries. Embark on an exhilarating journey as explore the mystique of Mount Kailash's spiritual significance, the enigmatic Bermuda Triangle's tales of disappearances, and the legendary lost city of Atlantis. This book unearths ancient legends, modern investigations, and theories that shroud these place..Join us in uncovering the hidden truths, speculation, and wonder that surround these captivating phenomena."

Also by Jagdish Krishanlal Arora

From Oasis to Global Stage: The Evolution of Arab Civilization
भगवत गीता
How to End The War in Ukraine
The Old and New World Order